Archaeology

Clare Goff

Macdonald/Educational

Managing Editor Chris Milsome
Editor Verity Weston
Editorial Assistant and
Picture Research Ruth Levenberg
Design and Research Sarah Tyzack
and Peter Benoist
Production Philip Hughes

First published 1973
Macdonald and Co (Publishers) Limited
St Giles House, 49–50 Poland Street
London W1A 2LG

contents

ISBN 0 356 04345 2

What is archaeology?

Digging for the past

An archaeologist is somebody who tries to discover how people lived in the past by studying the things they have left behind them. Sometimes huge buildings are still standing, like the Egyptian pyramids.

More often the ruins of ancient towns have become overgrown, covered with earth and forgotten. The archaeologist has to dig them up again and as he does so he recreates the past from tiny clues, rather like a detective.

Early treasure hunters

It is only recently that scholars have realized that it is possible to learn about the past in this way.

The first archaeologists were daring adventurers. They travelled through the jungles of central America or the deserts of the Middle East, rediscovering lost cities. They were sometimes attacked by bandits or imprisoned by local rulers.

Their work was not very scientific. They were only interested in the more spectacular parts of a civilization, such as its palaces and tombs. They also looked for works of art, such as Cleopatra's Needle, which could be shipped back home and sold to museums.

Archaeology today

Today all this has changed. A modern archaeologist tries to recover every detail of the day-to-day life of the people he is studying. He finds out about their houses, furniture and cooking pots, what animals they hunted and which crops they grew.

Archaeology has become scientific instead of just being a treasure hunt. However, this does not mean that digging is now dull.

▲ In the last century adventurers like Giovanni Belzoni shipped hundreds of valuable antiquities from the East to Europe. Here Belzoni is sending a head of Ramasses II to London.

Voyage of the *Cleopatra*

▲ Cleopatra's Needle is a huge obelisk 68½ feet (21 m.) high and weighing 186 tons. For centuries it lay in the sand, too heavy to move.

Then in 1877 British engineers encased it in a metal cylinder. A deck was built on top and a tug towed it back to England. The map shows the route of its voyage.

▶ Cleopatra's Needle now stands by the River Thames in London.

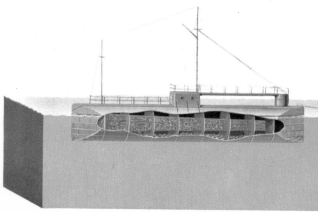

The *Cleopatra*, the ship built around Cleopatra's Needle, is towed by a tug. The *Cleopatra* was almost lost in a storm off the coast of Spain. She was only saved when a heavier steamer came to help.

Buried alive Pompeii and Herculaneum

The eruption of Mount Vesuvius

Pompeii and Herculaneum were fashionable sea-side towns in the Roman Empire, lying below Mount Vesuvius in southern Italy. On August 24th, 79 AD the people who lived there were just about to have dinner when there was a terrifying crash. Vesuvius had erupted!

Herculaneum was overwhelmed by a river of boiling mud which filled up the houses and then hardened. This preserved everything in the houses. Even the food on the tables was found in its original position. Luckily, most of the inhabitants had time to escape.

The people of Pompeii were not so fortunate. Many decided to wait and collect their valuables, or hide in their cellars until the eruption was over. They were overcome by fumes of poisonous sulphur and then smothered by ash.

The cities are uncovered

The cities remained undisturbed until 1709 when the local Italian princes began tunnelling through the ruins. They wanted to find bronze and marble statues to decorate their palaces.

Then some of the architects in charge of the excavations realized that here was a marvellous chance to see how the ancient Romans had really lived. They began to dig out the houses one by one and record everything they found inside them. This was the beginning of archaeology as we know it.

Today the excavations still continue. If you visit the cities, you can walk down the streets and into the houses and imagine what it was like to be an ancient Roman.

▲ One of the people left behind in Herculaneum was a 14-year-old boy whose legs may have been paralyzed. He was in bed about to eat chicken for lunch.

His mother had been working beside him on a loom. Perhaps she rushed into the street for help and got carried away by the panic-stricken mob. Her son must have lain there, helpless, watching the mud getting higher and higher.

▶ This is how Pompeii looks today.

A dog from Pompeii died fighting to get loose from its chain and was smothered by ashes.

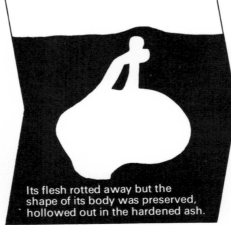

Its flesh rotted away but the shape of its body was preserved, hollowed out in the hardened ash.

The Italian archaeologist, Fiorelli, poured plaster into the hollow space left by the dog.

A Pompeiian house

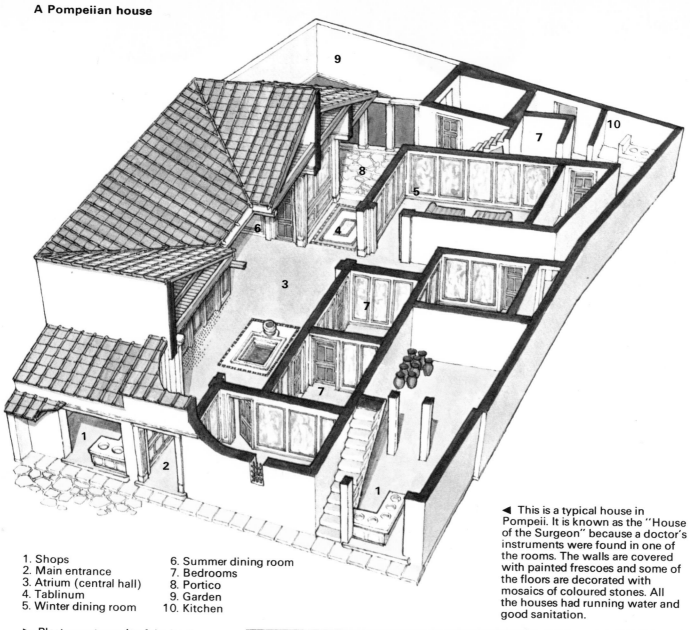

1. Shops
2. Main entrance
3. Atrium (central hall)
4. Tablinum
5. Winter dining room
6. Summer dining room
7. Bedrooms
8. Portico
9. Garden
10. Kitchen

◄ This is a typical house in Pompeii. It is known as the "House of the Surgeon" because a doctor's instruments were found in one of the rooms. The walls are covered with painted frescoes and some of the floors are decorated with mosaics of coloured stones. All the houses had running water and good sanitation.

▶ Plaster casts made of the bodies of people show how they died trying to escape. This man collapsed just as he reached the city gate.

This gave a perfect cast of the dog. In the same way casts were made of scores of other bodies.

5

The mask of Agamemnon

▲ Heinrich Schliemann, the German business man, began by earning £9 a year. He nearly died in a shipwreck but finally became an archaeologist.

▲ Schliemann's wife, Sophia, is wearing the "jewels of Helen" from Troy. Schliemann smuggled them out of Troy illegally.

▶ In one Shaft Grave, Schliemann found the bodies of three warriors, their faces protected by golden masks. When the masks were raised two of the skulls crumbled away but the face of the third man was perfectly preserved. His lips were slightly apart as if he was smiling.

Schliemann kissed the mask and then sent a telegram to the king of Greece: "I have gazed on the face of Agamemnon".

Schliemann believes Homer

One of the world's most famous archaeologists was Heinrich Schliemann. As a boy he had heard the tales of the Greek poet Homer about Troy.

Homer tells how Paris, Prince of Troy, ran off with Helen, wife of King Menelaus. Menelaus's brother, Agamemnon, king of Mycenae, raised an army of Greek heroes to get Helen back. After a ten year siege they finally captured Troy by entering the city in a hollow wooden horse.

Although the sites of Troy and Mycenae were well known, scholars did not believe that Homer's stories about them were true. Schliemann decided to prove that the scholars were wrong.

First he needed money. Having worked for a grocer, then as a cabin boy, he taught himself seven languages and went into business. At 46 he was a millionaire and free to fulfil his life's ambition.

Discoveries at Troy and Mycenae

Schliemann's first excavations at Troy were not very scientific. He thought that everything he found must belong to the time of Paris and Helen. Later excavations have shown that the Troy Paris knew was actually the seventh city to be built on the site. It had suffered a long siege before being captured and sacked, so there *was* truth in the legend.

From Troy, Schliemann turned to Mycenae and discovered the Shaft Graves. These were royal tombs filled with treasures very like those described by Homer.

Schliemann was sure that he had found the bodies of Agamemnon and his companions. We know now, however, that the Shaft Graves were dug about 200 years before the time of the Trojan War. If Agamemnon really lived, he may have been buried at Mycenae in one of the huge beehive tombs in the valley below the city wall.

The Shaft Graves in this grave circle at Mycenae were deep rectangular pits hollowed out just inside the citadel wall. They were surrounded by a circle of stone slabs which were later buried. Schliemann discovered five graves which contained the bodies of 19 people. These were laden with jewels and beside them were many beautiful objects.

▲ In one of the graves was a two-handled goblet of gold, with doves perching on the rim. It is known now as "Nestor's Cup" because Homer described a cup like this that belonged to the hero Nestor.

▲ Bronze daggers, inlaid with gold and silver, show Greek warriors carrying huge shields like the ones described by Homer.

► The "Treasury of Atreus" was obviously once the tomb of a hero, perhaps of Agamemnon himself. The huge underground chamber was about 50 feet (15 m.) across.

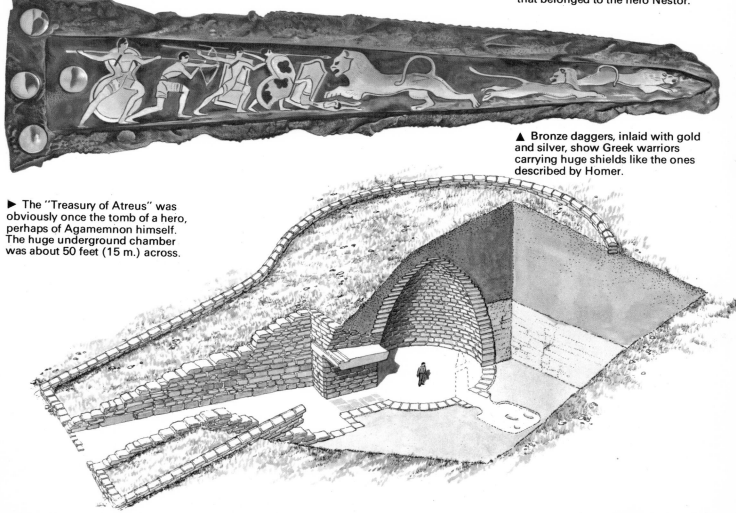

Mummies and pyramids

▲ This is the burial chamber in Tutankhamun's tomb at Thebes. His body still lies in the golden coffin inside the stone sarcophagus. The wall paintings show the dead king and funeral customs.

Egyptian burial customs

The civilization of Ancient Egypt flourished from about 3100 BC for thousands of years. We know a great deal about it, mainly because of the Egyptian beliefs about life after death. An Egyptian nobleman believed that when he died his spirit would go on living as comfortably as he had lived during his lifetime.

Because of this, his body had to be mummified so that his spirit could return to it whenever it wished. All his furniture and possessions had to be buried with him and the walls of his tomb would be decorated with scenes from his everyday life.

Archaeologists learn about Egypt

Archaeologists can use these pictures to find out about the day to day life of the Egyptian people. There are, for instance, pictures of nobles hunting ducks, going for pleasure cruises down the River Nile or just relaxing at home with their wives and children.

Development of the pyramids

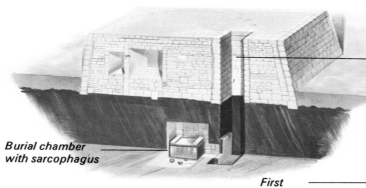

Burial shaft filled with sand and rubble

Burial chamber with sarcophagus

First four-step pyramid

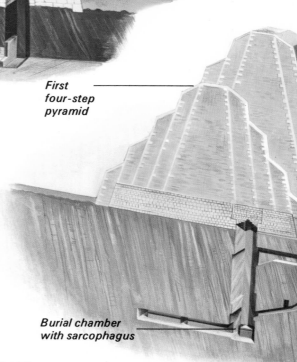

Burial chamber with sarcophagus

▲ 1. The first Egyptians were buried in pits surrounded by jars containing food and drink. The dry sand preserved their bodies, which may have suggested to them that bodies should be mummified. The grave was covered by a small mound, the ancestor of the pyramid.

▲ 2. After about 3100 BC the mound became a brick building, called a mastaba, imitating a house. The burial chamber was at first inside the mastaba, but later it was hidden at the bottom of a deep shaft. Decorated chapels were added round the sides.

▶ 3. The Step Pyramid of King Zoser dates from about 2683 BC. The king's architect, Imhotep, started by building a mastaba but kept on enlarging it until the base was 411 × 358 feet (125 × 109 m.). It was the largest building in the world at that time.

Tombs and robbers

The tombs of the Pharaohs and nobles contained so much treasure that the early kings were buried inside huge pyramids, for fear of robbers. Later, tombs were put in chambers at the end of long passages carved out of the limestone cliffs near Thebes.

In spite of all the efforts made to guard these tombs, most of them were plundered soon after they were built. In the last century rich collectors completed the damage, taking nearly all that remained. Only the tomb of Tutankhamun had not been discovered.

Tutankhamun's tomb

Tutankhamun was a boy of nine when he became king of Egypt and he was only 18 when he died in 1339 BC. His tomb was discovered in 1922 by Howard Carter after an eight-year search.

The tomb has allowed us to glimpse the wealth of objects once buried with all the Pharaohs. The archaeologists found gold chariots, gilded couches in the shape of bulls and hippos, and statues of the young king. There was also inlaid furniture including the chair the king used as a little boy. Even a wreath of spring flowers had been put there by his young wife.

▲ 4. The pyramid at Meidum was built in about 2600 BC. It began as a Step Pyramid too. Then it was smoothed over with limestone.

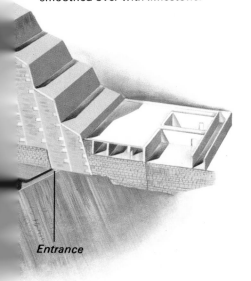

Entrance

Tutankhamun's head

◄ The Egyptians believed that if the body perished, the soul died with it, so they preserved bodies by mummifying them. First the brain was removed through the nostrils, and the liver, lungs and intestines were taken out.

Then the body was soaked for 70 days in a dehydrating liquid. Finally it was bandaged and ointments were poured over it.

Tutankhamun's face had been protected by a beautiful portrait mask but the rest of his body had rotted away.

Operation on a mummy

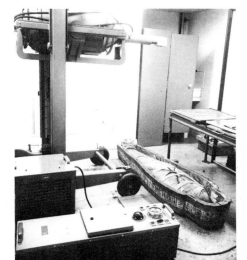

◄ 1. X-raying mummies is a good way of studying them without unwrapping all the bandages. X-rays show the state of the dead man's body and whether there are any jewels hidden among the bindings.

Here the mummy of Hor, a priest of Amun who lived in about 800 BC, is about to be photographed. He lies in a gaily painted mummy-shaped coffin.

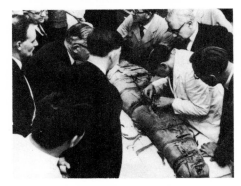

◄ 2. The X-ray shows that there is a statue lying between Hor's legs, so a cut is made in the wrappings to reach it. The X-ray also shows that he died in middle age, that most of his upper teeth are missing, and that his own eyes have been replaced by artificial ones.

◄ 3. The statue turns out to be a stone *ushabti* figure. The Egyptians believed that their spirits might be forced to run errands for the gods or to labour in their fields in the afterlife. *Ushabtis* were buried in the tombs to be their servants and do this work for them.

Archaeologists in action work on a dig

▲ Excavations are always run by trained archaeologists, but most of the digging is done by workmen or student volunteers. Here students dig through the layers of a Roman road.

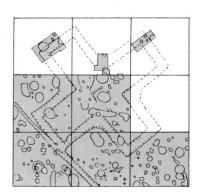

▲ Archaeologists make two kinds of drawing for each site. A horizontal plan is like a scale map of the site. This one, of part of a hill fort, shows the foundations of an early church cutting across earlier storage pits.

Plans and sections

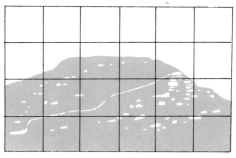

▲ The other kind of drawing is called a section. It is drawn from the side of a trench and gives a vertical picture of the layers of a site. This section through the hill fort's defences shows that they were rebuilt at least three times.

Buildings of different levels

Excavation methods have become more scientific since the days of Schliemann. To understand how a modern archaeologist works it is useful to see how a town grows up over the years.

People often go on living in the same place for a very long time. In years gone by, when a house fell down the inhabitants just smoothed over the rubble and built a new building on top. Fortification walls were often rebuilt on a much grander scale using the earlier walls as a base.

In this way, the floors and stumps of walls from really early structures are often preserved beneath the foundations of later ones. (There is a picture showing this on page 20.)

Methods of excavation

The archaeologist tackles this type of site level by level. He lays out a plan for digging trenches, usually in the form of a rectangular framework or "grid" and then starts stripping off the turf and topsoil. The closer he gets to the ancient buildings, the more cautiously he has to proceed.

As the stumps of the old walls emerge from the soil they are cleaned, planned and photographed. Any finds from the floors of the houses are collected in labelled trays.

Then the excavators move on to the level below. The sides of the trenches are kept as straight as possible and eventually give a complete cross-section of the settlement, showing how the various building levels have been added on.

At the end of the season a report on the dig is published. It contains drawings to scale of these cross-sections, or sections, as well as plans of the buildings.

Excavating sites of wooden houses

In northern Europe, and North America, where people built houses of wood, often little remains of a settlement. There might only be rings of postholes marking the position of houses, and rubbish pits.

The various "levels" are so thin and lie so close together, that they are hard to distinguish. The excavators have to go very slowly and notice the way the postholes and pits cut into each other to find out which structures or buildings were built first.

Tools for excavation

▲ First a tape-measure, pegs and tapes are needed for laying out the trenches and heavy digging tools for removing the turf and topsoil.

▲ Delicate tools, such as small picks and builders' trowels, are used for excavating the ancient structures themselves.

▲ The excavated structures are cleaned up with trowels and brushes and then planned and photographed.

Dig director's caravan

Metric staff

Level

This picture shows a typical dig in Europe. One girl is drawing a plan of the side of a trench. Her plan will show a cross-section similar to the one on the opposite page.

Further back two people are using a level and a metric staff to find the accurate height of objects that are uncovered. The excavator can be used for removing large amounts of top soil.

▲ Finds from a dig are put into labelled trays, a separate tray for each area and level. They are then washed and labelled with the place where they were found.

Behind the scenes restoring finds

▲ These Greek technicians are repairing pots from the Agora at Athens. First they carefully stick all the pieces together. Then the missing sections are filled with plaster of Paris which can be painted to look like the rest of the pot.

The restoration of objects

Not all the objects found on an excavation are as well preserved as those from Herculaneum or Tutankhamun's tomb. In most sites they have been lying in the damp earth for hundreds or thousands of years. They have either rotted away completely or are in very poor shape indeed when they are eventually uncovered.

Pots are often smashed to pieces and have to be stuck back carefully together again. Some metals rust badly and have to be cleaned and chemically treated.

Materials such as wood, cloth and leather that come from plants and animals are the most difficult of all to deal with. They are only preserved in very unusual circumstances, for example, in a very dry desert, a waterlogged bog, or a tightly-sealed tomb. When they are brought into the fresh air they quickly begin to crumble away to nothing and have to be protected with hot wax or liquid plastic.

Usually, only emergency treatments take place on the site of the excavation. Proper cleaning and restoration work takes place later back in the museum laboratories. Finally the restored pots, weapons and jewellery are drawn and photographed for the excavation report. Then they are put on display in a museum.

Reconstruction of the Mars Sword

▲ 1. Treatment starts at the British Museum on a badly corroded Roman sword from South Shields. The blade looks like a lump of rust.

▲ 2. An X-ray shows that it was built up of thick wires of iron and steel. These were forged together for strength with inlays of golden bronze.

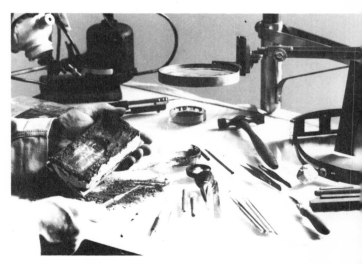

▲ 3. The technician uses a drill and other dental tools. He removes the rust from the blade as a dentist removes decay from a tooth.

The cleaned blade is then encased in transparent plastic. This makes the decorative bronze inlays easier to see.

▶ The court ladies of Ur wore gold and silver jewellery set with beads of blue lapis and red carnelian.

A court lady of Ur

The royal tombs of Ur

Some of the most fascinating objects ever discovered came from the royal tombs at Ur in southern Mesopotamia. The tombs were built just before 2500 BC and were excavated by Sir Leonard and Lady Woolley in 1926.

The kings and queens had been buried surrounded by up to 74 members of their court. These attendants had been sacrificed. They had apparently followed their royal masters down into the tomb where they were all drugged. There were also many treasures: gold and silver harps, golden cups, weapons and statues.

All these beautiful objects, together with the wonderful head-dresses of the court ladies, had been crushed flat under the weight of the earth. Often the gold, mother of pearl or lapis inlaid decoration had been fitted into a wooden framework which had rotted away. Only the position of the inlaid stones, lying loose in the earth, showed that the object they came from must have been a harp or a chariot.

Woolley had to solidify everything with hot paraffin wax before the objects could be removed for further treatment. Then the wooden framework was carved afresh, the wax gently melted and the jewellery carefully cleaned and remounted in its new setting.

▲ 4. One side has an eagle between military standards.

▶ 5. The other side shows Mars, the war god.

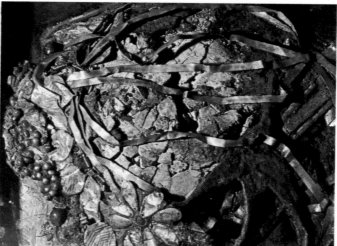

▲ The crushed skull and head-dress of a court lady looked like this when it was found. By carefully noting the position of each bead Woolley managed to put the head-dress together again.

Secrets from bogs past environments

How peat deposits are formed: the story of a lake in northern Europe

Pre-Boreal 8300-7500 BC

As the Ice Age glaciers begin to retreat north, lakes form from the melting water, full of reeds and water-lilies. Birch trees and willows start to grow in the barren tundra.

A family group camps by the side of the lake. They are able to live by hunting red-deer, elk and small game.

Boreal 7500-5000 BC

As the weather improves, pine trees and then dense thickets of hazel replace the birches. The men have now mastered the new conditions.

They chop down trees to build houses and boats, and fish with lines and nets. They also shoot wild fowl with arrows, and they tame wolves to guard the camp at night.

Atlantic 5000-3000 BC

The weather is warm and wet and thick forests cover the countryside. The lake no longer provides any fish, as it is choked with reeds and rotting vegetation.

The tribe migrates to the coast and lives on shell fish, fowling and deep sea fishing. Then, some time before 3000 BC, farming is introduced from the East.

Sub-Boreal 3000-600 BC

Men return and burn or chop down the forest to provide land for farming and fodder for cattle. Pollen from cornflowers and sorrel, and from bracken that grows on the burnt clearings, blows on to the old lake bed.

This has now become peaty pasture where cattle graze, unaware of the story lying beneath their feet.

Changes in man's environment

Before 10,000 BC, northern Europe, parts of Asia and North America were covered by huge ice sheets. Mammoth, reindeer, bison and other big game roamed the tundra to the south and were hunted by Cave men and Paleo Indians.

Then, shortly before 8,000 BC, the climate began to improve. The ice retreated northwards to the Pole. Forests of birch, then evergreens like spruce and pine replaced the tundra. Then came hardwoods like oak, ash and elm and, in America, chestnut and hickory.

The big game animals died out and were replaced by smaller forms of deer and other woodland animals. To cope with these new conditions, men had drastically to alter their hunting methods and way of life.

The secret of peat

The story of all these changes lies buried in the ancient lake beds of northern Europe and America. It was discovered by Swedish geologists who studied Scandinavian peat bogs. Peat consists of the remains of dead plants. It is collected in the shallow water of ancient lakes layer upon layer, like the levels of a dig.

If you look at a sample of prehistoric peat under a microscope you will see that it contains thousands of pollen grains. These came from the trees and plants that were growing round the lake when the peat bogs were forming.

By studying the different types of pollen in a peat sample, scientists can tell what the countryside was like at the time the peat was formed. If they take a series of samples from top to bottom of a lake they can also work out how the vegetation and climate changed from one period to the next.

▲ Peat bogs can preserve people as well as pollen. In Denmark, peat-cutters have dug up the naked bodies of men, women and children. They had been strangled or had had their throats cut before being drowned in the bog.

These victims had usually lived on herb gruel before they died so they may have been criminals, or sacrifices to the Earth goddess. Tollund Man's peaceful expression suggests that he was a good man who accepted his fate willingly.

◄ This man was found in another Danish bog in 1892. He was lying just as he had been buried 2000 years earlier.

The first farmers

▼ Chatal Huyuk was a mud-brick town over 8,000 years old in central Turkey. It was probably a holy city, for the walls of the houses were covered with paintings and sculptures mainly of birth, death and hunting.

The beginning of farming

The first farmers lived in the fertile hilly country around the eastern Mediterranean. They started by following herds of wild sheep and goats which roamed the area, and collecting the seeds of wild wheat and barley.

Gradually people learnt how to tame the younger animals and sow corn in clearings near their camps. Once this happened (around 7000 BC) they no longer had to move around after the herds, but could settle in villages.

Because life was so much easier, the cleverer villagers had time to experiment. They painted frescoes on the walls of their houses, spun and dyed wool for rugs and clothing and made vessels of stone and clay.

Farming spread rapidly from the Middle East into Europe and central Asia, but in the New World, the Indians made the same discoveries for themselves. Of course different animals and plants were used in different areas. In the East people grew rice, in the Americas they grew maize and potatoes. In Peru they tamed the llama, in India the elephant and buffalo, in Russia the horse, and everywhere—the dog.

▲ These foundations are of a 7,000 year old farm-house from Hacilar in southern Turkey. Notice the holes that held the posts supporting the roof, the plastered fire-place and hearth, and the storage niches in the walls.

▼ This flint dagger, found at Chatal Huyuk, may have been used for religious sacrifices.

▶ Modern farmers' houses are still built in much the same way with mud-brick walls and flat roofs.

▲ The vultures devouring the headless bodies in the wall paintings have human legs. Perhaps they represent priests, dressed up as birds, in charge of burial rites, as the picture suggests. Dead bodies were always exposed outside the village and their bodies picked clean by vultures before they were brought home and buried under the house floors.

◄ Middle Eastern villagers still use many of the old farming methods. Here a farmer threshes his corn by driving a sledge round and round a pile of wheat.

A prehistoric deep freeze in Siberia

Scythian burial chambers

The Scythians lived on the steppes of central Asia in the first millenium BC. They were nomadic tribesmen who bred horses and cattle.

The Greek historian Herodotus wrote that when a chief died his followers embalmed the corpse and carried it in procession through tribal territories. Then a funeral chamber of logs was built at the bottom of a deep pit.

The chief's body was placed inside, together with his wife, horses and sometimes his servants. Finally a huge mound was piled up over the grave.

Excavations carried out at Pazyryk in the Altai mountains on the Chinese-Russian border show that Herodotus was right. Russian archaeologists discovered a group of high mounds covering underground log tombs.

The ground directly below the mounds had frozen and the tombs, opened by grave robbers, had been flooded and were filled with solid ice.

Frozen treasure

This ice had preserved the bodies of the chieftains and their wives and their horses for 2,400 years, as if in a giant deep freeze. With them, too, were their clothes and personal belongings, the felt hangings and carpets that decorated the chambers, and the gay saddle cloths and bridles of the horses.

The Russians had to thaw out the tombs with buckets of hot water before they could excavate. They found that the best preserved burials were tombs two and five.

The chief in tomb two had been killed in battle when about 60 and had been scalped by the enemy before his followers got his body back. They had given him a false scalp and a beard of horse hair and had replaced his brain and entrails with herbs.

His young wife had a long black pigtail. She wore a mantle of squirrel fur, an apron trimmed with otter and sable and embroidered felt boots.

▲ Horses wore elaborate masks of leather and fur for the funeral procession.

▲ A Greek vase shows how Scythians dressed in wool tunics, trousers and boots.

Frozen ground

▲ A cross-section through a tomb shows the chamber built of a double thickness of logs. You can see the tomb shaft, the huge mound of rubble covering the entrance and the hole made by tomb robbers when they broke in.

The mound protected the layer of earth lying directly below it from the sun. Because of this the tomb and all its contents were frozen solid and preserved intact.

▲ A felt wall hanging from tomb five shows a Scythian chief and horseman.

▲ The body of the chief in tomb two had weird animals tattooed on it.

◄ When the tombs were excavated the bodies and their possessions were found scattered all over the floor, just as the robbers had left them. This is how burial two may have looked just after the funeral.

The walls were lined with black felt. The bodies of the chief and his wife lay in a tree-trunk coffin. Seven horses lay in a separate room.

◄ This is what the funeral procession of tomb five may have looked like. The horses were chestnut or brown geldings.

They wore brilliant saddle cloths and their bridles were decorated with wooden animals covered with gold foil. Some of them wore elaborate masks which were crowned with antlers.

The wagon had felt hangings. It may have come from China as a bridal dowry.

Dating the past

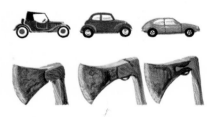

▲ **Typology.** The sports car is clearly later than the veteran. Similarly, the second and third axes clearly developed from the first simple axe.

▼ In the Middle East, sites are occupied for so long that there may be the remains of 20 or more mud-brick villages built one above the other. These form a small hill, called a "tell", which rises above the surface of the plain.

Here a trench through the upper levels of a small mound in Persia shows how the pottery changes four times in a few hundred years. The levels can be dated to within 100 years by C14 samples taken from the various floors.

Stone, bronze and iron

How can one date things from the past when there is no written history? The first person to try was Christian Thomsen in the Danish National Museum.

He suddenly realized that the ancient objects made of stone seemed to be earlier and more primitive than those made of metal. He also found that tools and weapons of copper and bronze seemed to come before those of iron. In 1836 he suggested that the period before written history could be divided into three ages: Stone, Bronze and Iron.

These periods were first divided up by "typology". The archaeologist compares objects and supposes that complicated types of tools and weapons came later than simpler ones. It was safer, however to use the evidence from digs.

Pottery

In many parts of the world people often lived in the same place for a very long time. When an archaeologist digs down below the latest houses on a site, he finds the remains of earlier houses underneath.

The floors of the houses are covered with pieces of broken pottery. As the archaeologist digs deeper into the remains of even earlier settlements, the colour and shapes of the pots change.

On a really ancient site, like some of the towns in the Middle East, the pottery fashions can change many times as new people enter the town. An archaeologist knows in which order the various styles of pottery appear on one site. He can use them, therefore, to date levels on other sites in the same area.

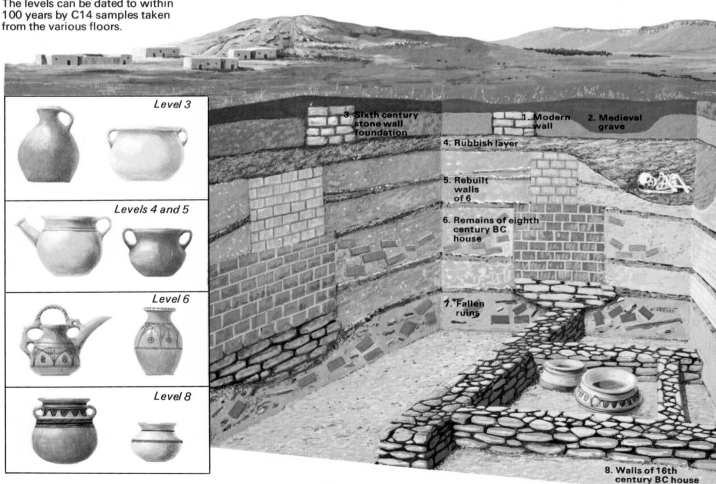

Level 3

Levels 4 and 5

Level 6

Level 8

3. Sixth century stone wall foundation

1. Modern wall

2. Medieval grave

4. Rubbish layer

5. Rebuilt walls of 6

6. Remains of eighth century BC house

7. Fallen ruins

8. Walls of 16th century BC house

Cross-section of a Persian mound

▲ The dated pots can be used to date similar levels from other sites.

Tree rings and carbon

Objects of stone, bronze, iron and pottery can only tell us the order in which things happened and not their actual dates. "Dendrochronology" means dating buildings by counting tree rings.

Dendrochronology was discovered by the American A. E. Douglass and it is used in the southern United States for dating Indian ruins. It will give the exact year a house was first built.

Elsewhere, archaeologists use radio-carbon dating, which was discovered by another American, W. Libby. He found that all living things absorb a small amount of radio-active carbon (C_{14}) from the atmosphere. When an animal or plant dies, the C_{14} in its body begins to disintegrate at a steady rate so that the quantity is halved in about 5,730 years.

Archaeologists extract carbon from an ancient piece of bone or charcoal and measure its radio-activity. Like this they can tell, within a few hundred years, how long ago it was buried.

Tree-ring dating

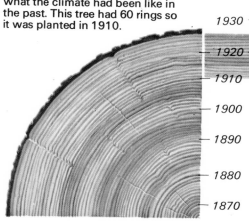

▶ **1.** Each year a tree grows a ring of new wood which is thicker in wet years than in dry ones. Douglass began counting the rings on stumps.

By doing this he could find out when the tree was planted and what the climate had been like in the past. This tree had 60 rings so it was planted in 1910.

◀ **2.** Douglass argued that every tree in an area is affected by the same cycle of wet and dry summers. Therefore they will all show wide and narrow rings in the same order.

This tree was cut down in 1925. so the *outer* rings on its trunk will match the *inner* rings of the first tree.

▲ Modern Indians in the south-western United States still live in houses very similar to those of several hundred years ago.

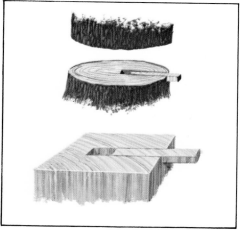

◀ **3.** To push his tree calendar back even further, Douglass looked for beams from old houses and archaeological sites. He developed a special drill to take borings from the beams just big enough for their rings to be counted. In this way he was able to date buildings back as far as 11 AD.

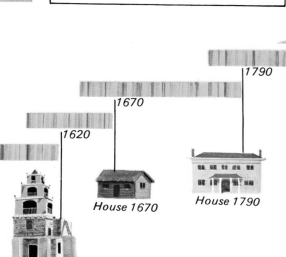

1973

1890

Tree cut down in 1973

1850

Old Tree stump 1890

House 1850

1790

1670

House 1790

1620

House 1670

1500

Spanish church 1620

Pueblo houses 1500

▲ **4.** Once Douglass had constructed his calendar it could be used to date any new archaeological site discovered in the southern United States. One just had to find a beam, draw out its ring pattern, and then find the matching section in the calendar. Here tree rings date old houses, a church and a pueblo (town).

Breaking the code ancient scripts

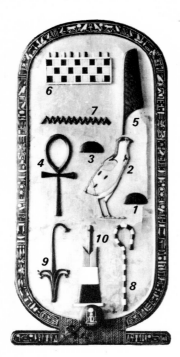

▲ The signs in the cartouche of Tutankhamun are: 1-3 = TUT (Image), 4 = Ankh (Symbol of Life), 5-7 = Y MN N (Amun), so 1-7 read TUT-ANKH-AMUN, which means The Living Image of Amun (Amun was a god).

8 = Ruler, 9 = Southern and 10 = On, so 8-10 say The Ruler of Southern On (a part of Thebes).

▼ **The hieroglyphic alphabet.** The original meanings are under the pictures; the sounds that the pictures came to represent are above.

Ancient writing

Dating the past is much easier when people leave written records such as building inscriptions, letters and lists of kings. The two earliest forms of writing were invented just before 3000 BC in Egypt and Mesopotamia, but many other peoples also made up scripts of their own.

Most of these early forms of writing were very clumsy and went out of use when the alphabet was invented. So when the first ancient inscriptions were rediscovered no one knew how to read them. Now most have been deciphered.

Egyptian hieroglyphs

The Egyptians started to write by drawing pictures. PER "house" was written ⊏⊐ : and RO "mouth" ⊂⊃ . Then the pictures started to stand for the *sounds* of the words too. ⊏⊐ could also be read "PR" and ⊂⊃ "R".

Although they had an alphabet, however, the Egyptians went on using the older picture and syllable signs alongside it. They even added extra signs to indicate what sort of a word was being written, e.g. PERY "to go out" was spelt ⊟ 𐦢 𐦢 ∧ . The "walking legs" show it is a word of action.

How the hieroglyphs were deciphered

In 1798 Napoleon invaded Egypt and scholars began bringing inscriptions to Europe. Jean-François Champollion, a French schoolboy, was fascinated by the hieroglyphs and determined to translate them. He began learning eastern languages and by the age of 16 could read six, including Coptic, a form of ancient Egyptian.

Several of the inscriptions, such as the Rosetta stone and an obelisk from Philae were written in two languages: Greek and Egyptian.

Champollion found that the hieroglyphs in oval frames or "cartouches" indicated the name of a king.

In one of the cartouches, correspond-

ing to the name Ptolemy in the Greek, the first, third and fourth signs were the same as the fifth, fourth and second signs of the cartouche of Cleopatra. Therefore they surely stood for the letters P, O and L. If so, the sixth and ninth signs of Cleopatra stood for A.

Champollion filled in the missing letters and used them to decipher several other cartouches. Soon he had discovered the whole alphabet. But the older names were different. One was ⊙ 𐦢 ⌒⌒ . He knew that the last signs were SS. The first could be a picture of the sun, in Coptic "Ra". If so the second might be MS or Mas, the Coptic word for "birth". This gave Ramasses "Child of the Sun", the hard-hearted Pharaoh of the Bible.

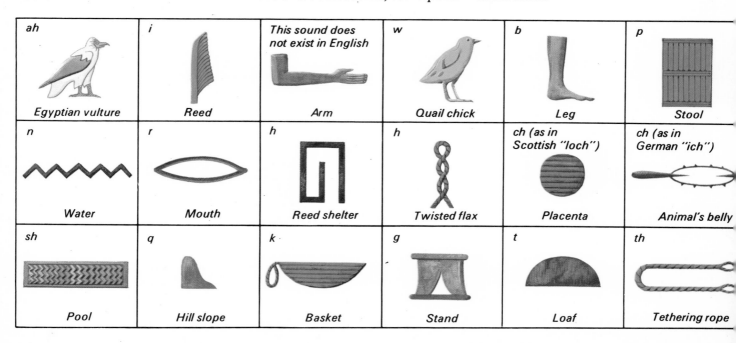

ah	i	This sound does not exist in English	w	b	p
Egyptian vulture	Reed	Arm	Quail chick	Leg	Stool
n	r	h	h	ch (as in Scottish "loch")	ch (as in German "ich")
Water	Mouth	Reed shelter	Twisted flax	Placenta	Animal's belly
sh	q	k	g	t	th
Pool	Hill slope	Basket	Stand	Loaf	Tethering rope

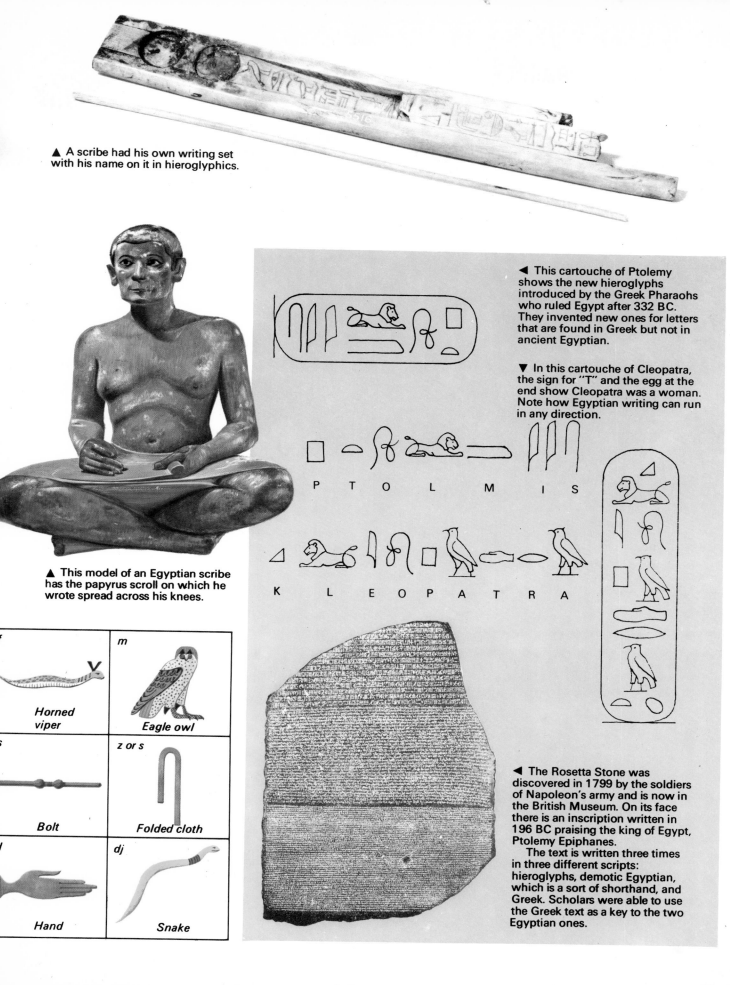

▲ A scribe had his own writing set with his name on it in hieroglyphics.

▲ This model of an Egyptian scribe has the papyrus scroll on which he wrote spread across his knees.

◄ This cartouche of Ptolemy shows the new hieroglyphs introduced by the Greek Pharaohs who ruled Egypt after 332 BC. They invented new ones for letters that are found in Greek but not in ancient Egyptian.

▼ In this cartouche of Cleopatra, the sign for "T" and the egg at the end show Cleopatra was a woman. Note how Egyptian writing can run in any direction.

P T O L M Is

K L E O P A T R A

f	m
Horned viper	Eagle owl
s	z or s
Bolt	Folded cloth
d	dj
Hand	Snake

◄ The Rosetta Stone was discovered in 1799 by the soldiers of Napoleon's army and is now in the British Museum. On its face there is an inscription written in 196 BC praising the king of Egypt, Ptolemy Epiphanes.
The text is written three times in three different scripts: hieroglyphs, demotic Egyptian, which is a sort of shorthand, and Greek. Scholars were able to use the Greek text as a key to the two Egyptian ones.

Treasures from the sea

► This bronze statue of a jockey from the third century BC was found in the sea near Cape Artemision in Greece.

Depth ga

Air tanks —

Knife

Weig
belt

Telephor

Meta

Diving for ancient wrecks

One of the most exciting forms of archaeology is looking for ancient wrecks under the sea. An underwater archaeologist has two main problems to face: lack of air and increasing pressure from the water the deeper he dives.

He stays alive by using an aqualung. This provides him with air from tanks on his back equal in pressure to the water surrounding him. Even so, if he goes below about 100 feet (30 m.) his brain is affected from breathing in too much pressurized nitrogen.

He has to return to the surface very slowly or paralyzing bubbles will form in his blood.

New methods

All this means that a diver can only spend a short time each day on the wreck and new methods have to be invented to speed up the work. Most of the planning is done by photography as there is no time to make drawings.

The American, George Bass, has invented a miniature submarine equipped with cameras. It can work at great depths and photograph and plan a sunken cargo in an hour.

The Frenchman, Jacques Cousteau, has built underwater "villages" of air-filled balloons where men can live for a whole month. Future excavations could be run from such villages.

Treasures from the Armada

▲ These golden jewels came from a Spanish ship wrecked off Northern Ireland.

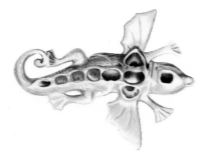

▲ Spanish sailors wore jewelled salamanders, like this one, to protect them against fire.

▲ This gold box shaped like a book could have been used for make-up or poison.

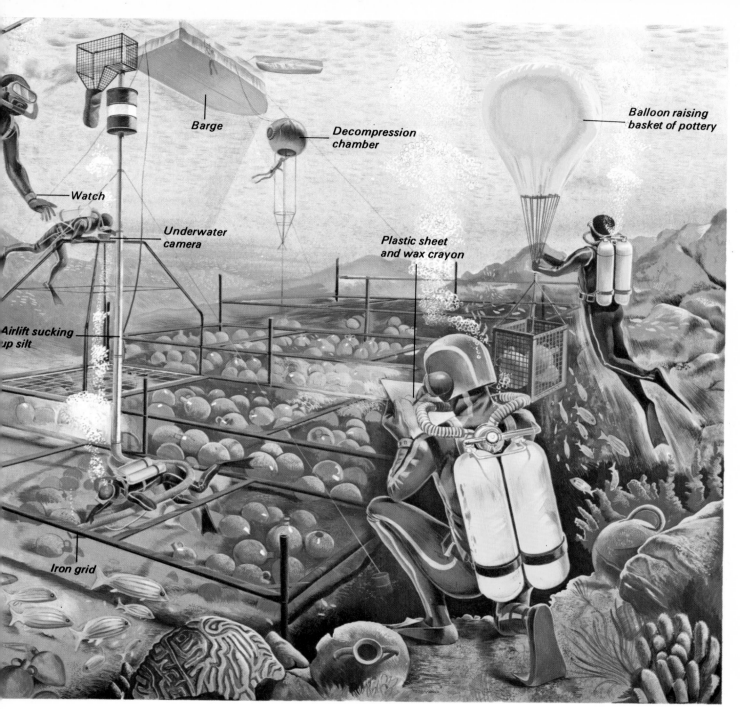

Barge

Decompression chamber

Balloon raising basket of pottery

Watch

Underwater camera

Plastic sheet and wax crayon

Airlift sucking up silt

Iron grid

▼ Objects from the wreck at Yassi Ada include gold coins of the Emperor Heraclius, who reigned between 610-641 BC.

▲ **An underwater excavation**
This picture shows some of the methods used by George Bass at Yassi Ada off the Turkish coast. He was excavating a Byzantine merchant ship which had been carrying a cargo of wine when she ran aground.

An air lift, which works by suction rather like a vacuum cleaner, is removing sand and mud. A photographer takes pictures from a tower erected over the squares of a metal grid.

Wire baskets of finds are floated to the surface by balloon. Finally the ship's timbers will be brought to the surface and the ship will be rebuilt on land.

Ships on dry land the Vikings

▲ This dragon's head from Oseberg was probably the prow of a ship. The warrior is from Oseberg too.

▲ In 1880 the Gokstad ship was dug from the clay mound which had preserved her for over 1,000 years.

▶ The Oseberg ship had been plundered but she still contained the bones of an old lady as well as her possessions. The ship had obviously been a queen's pleasure barge for sailing the fiord in fine weather. Her prow and gunwhale are beautifully carved and contained a carved wagon and sledges for royal processions on land.

The Viking ships

It is much easier to reconstruct ancient ships if they are found on land. This sometimes happens, as with the Viking ship burials of Scandinavia.

The Vikings are usually thought of as raiders from Norway, Sweden and Denmark, who invaded the coasts of Europe from about 800 AD onwards. In fact they were also artists and poets who composed long dramatic poems called "sagas" about the journeys of their adventurous heroes.

The Vikings were merchants too. There were Viking trading stations right through central Russia, and Viking colonies in Normandy, the British Isles, Greenland and Iceland.

However, the Vikings were above all seafarers. Even their long houses were shaped like boats. When a Viking chief died he was often buried in his ship which was dragged ashore and then covered by a high mound.

The most famous of these ship burials come from Gokstad and Oseberg in Oslo fiord in southern Norway. The Oseberg ship is more beautifully carved but appears to be less seaworthy than the Gokstad ship.

The Gokstad ship

The Gokstad ship was the tomb of a gouty old warrior of 50. He was accompanied by 12 horses, six dogs and a peacock. He also had with him a tent with dragon-headed tent poles, five bedsteads, a sledge and cooking pots.

The ship was 76 feet (25·15 m.) long, but could float in just over three feet (one metre) of water. This would have been handy in a Viking raiding expedition up shallow rivers.

Did the Vikings reach America?

The Viking sagas tell us that in 986 AD several ships blown off course from Greenland reached a fertile country where grapes grew wild in summer. In 1893 the Swedes built an exact copy of the Gokstad ship and sailed her across the Atlantic in 27 days. This proved that the land the Vikings reached could have been North America.

Besides this, excavators at L'Anse aux Meadows in Newfoundland have discovered a typical Viking long house and a small forge for smelting iron. Since iron working was unknown to the Indians, this may be the site of a colony the Vikings tried to found.

A Viking warrior

◄ This iron spearhead was found buried in a grave at the great Viking base at Birka in Sweden.

▲ This axe was part of a hoard of weapons found near London Bridge. It came from a Viking battle ship.

▲ This is a carved head showing the cone-shaped helmet with a nose-piece which was worn by the later Vikings.

▲ This is one of the 64 shields from the Gokstad ship that were hung along the sides in harbour.

▲ William the Conqueror wore a helmet and coat of chain mail like this one found in the grave of a Viking warrior.

◄ Objects found by archaeologists help to provide a picture of what a Viking warrior probably looked like.
Information is also provided by written descriptions and tapestries. On the famous Bayeux tapestry the followers of William the Conqueror, who were descended from Vikings, are shown dressed like this and with similar weapons.

Spaniards in Mexico early anthropologists

▲ The Aztecs usually stacked the skulls of their victims on racks, but a few were kept and overlaid with turquoise mosaic. This one may represent the god Tezcatipoca.

When past meets present

In the past 500 years, explorers have often come upon primitive tribes still living in the way men did in the Stone and Bronze Ages. A study of these people shows how our ancestors might have lived and thought.

Scholars who do this work are called anthropologists. They often work closely with archaeologists studying primitive societies.

In the 16th century the Spaniards started exploring central America. They found a group of tribes dominated by the Aztecs who were still living as the Egyptians had 4,000 years before. They were ruled by a king, built pyramids, wrote in hieroglyphs and only worked in copper and gold.

The Spaniards were horrified because the Aztecs sacrificed human beings to their gods. They burnt down the Aztec capital, Tenochtitlan, and built Mexico City on its ruins. The Jesuits burnt the Aztec books and converted the Indians to Christianity.

But then the Spanish governors became interested in the people they were ruling. They employed Aztec scribes to write new books in hieroglyphs, with a Spanish translation, to describe the life of the Aztec people.

Modern archaeologists use these books to imagine what Tenochtitlan was like. The books also help them to understand the purpose of other pyramids and temples found in central America.

Palace of Axayacatl

Northern canoe basin

► This picture from an Aztec history book shows the Spaniards killing the Aztecs during a religious dance.

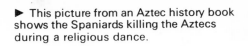

▼ Tenochtitlan was on an island and its roads were canals. In the centre was a pyramid with the temples of the sun and rain gods. Prisoners had their hearts cut out as a sacrifice to these gods. Their bodies were rolled down the side of the pyramid.

Temples to Huitzilopochtli and Tlaloc

Temple of Quetzalcoatl

School for training priests

Searching for sites lost Inca cities

▲ Hiram Bingham, the American explorer who rediscovered Machu Picchu, photographed outside his tent during an expedition.

The Inca Empire

One of the most interesting parts of an archaeologist's work is looking for new sites. Many parts of the world have already been thoroughly explored so one often has to travel long distances in difficult country by Land-Rover or on foot or horseback. Some of the most spectacular sites to have been discovered like this are the lost Inca cities of Peru.

The ancient Peruvians were clever farmers and engineers. They tamed llamas and developed many of the main foods and drugs we use today (for example, potatoes, chocolate, tomatoes and quinine).

In the 14th century AD the Incas built up a huge empire stretching for 3,000 miles along the Andes. It was held together by fortified towns linked by wide military highways.

In 1532, however, the Spanish adventurer Pizarro conquered the Incas. He captured the Great Inca, Atahualpa, by a trick. After the conquest one branch of the Inca royal family retreated to an isolated province called Vilcabamba and held out until 1572. Then Vilcabamba was conquered and its strongholds were abandoned and forgotten.

In 1911 a young American, Hiram Bingham, set out into the Andes to try to find the lost Inca cities. He had the old Spanish account of their last campaign and used it to try and retrace their route through the mountains.

He soon found several magnificent cities and shrines. The most spectacular was Machu Picchu and Bingham was sure (though many scholars disagree with him now) that he had discovered Vilcabamba itself.

▲ The Incas built with huge blocks of stone which they quarried and hoisted into position using only simple tools. This fortress is near Cuzco, the Inca capital.

▶ Machu Picchu consisted of a palace, barracks and private houses built between two mountain peaks. The inhabitants terraced the mountain sides to grow maize, squash and potatoes.

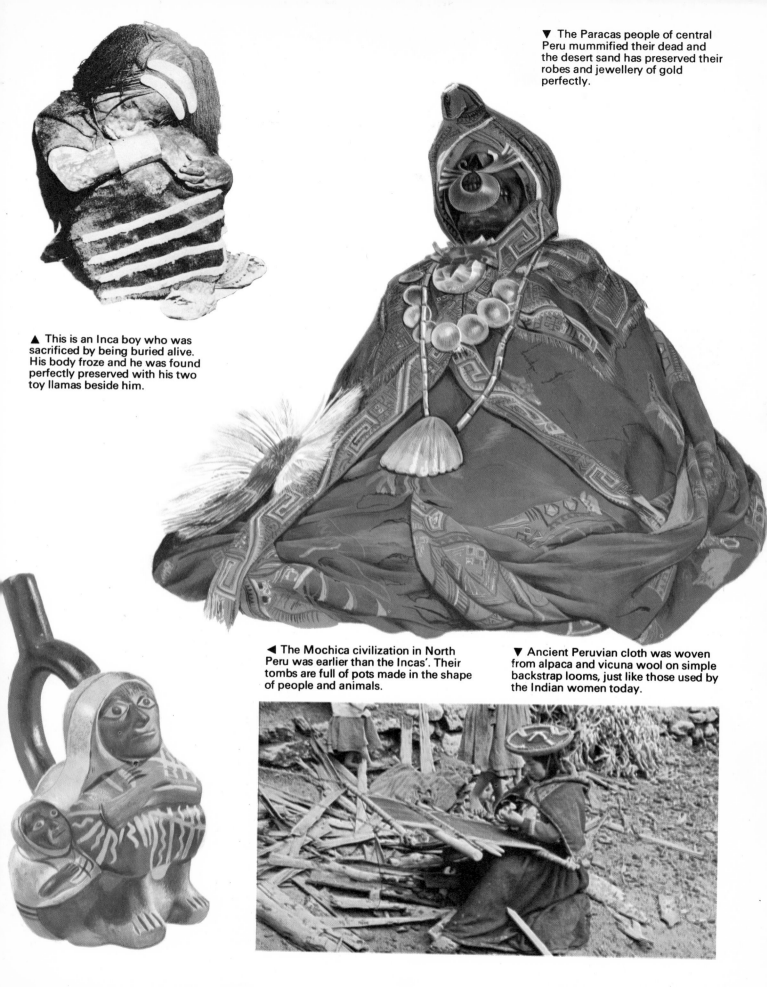

▼ The Paracas people of central Peru mummified their dead and the desert sand has preserved their robes and jewellery of gold perfectly.

▲ This is an Inca boy who was sacrificed by being buried alive. His body froze and he was found perfectly preserved with his two toy llamas beside him.

◄ The Mochica civilization in North Peru was earlier than the Incas'. Their tombs are full of pots made in the shape of people and animals.

▼ Ancient Peruvian cloth was woven from alpaca and vicuna wool on simple backstrap looms, just like those used by the Indian women today.

Seeing the invisible

Crop marks

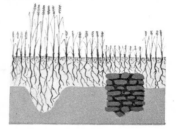

▲ Crops growing over buried walls lack moisture and grow stunted and yellow. Those planted over buried ditches grow high and green.

▲ A Roman villa shows up in the evening sun because the crops growing above the walls are shorter than their neighbours and lie in shadow.

Air photography

Modern archaeologists have a big advantage as they can use air photographs. From the air one can quickly survey wide sweeps of mountainous or desert countryside that would take weeks to explore properly on foot.

One can also get an overall view of the plans of towns or fortresses which, when seen close-to, look only like a maze of walls. Other types of sites that are practically invisible at ground level can be seen clearly from the air.

Low earth works, like field boundaries, sometimes show up in the early morning or late evening when the sun is low and casts long shadows. Other sites, buried below corn fields, show up as crop marks where the corn has grown greener or browner over buried ditches and walls.

Air photography was first developed for military purposes. Many countries are now covered by complete series of air photographs taken by their national air forces.

▲ In this air photograph of the Etruscan cemetery at Tarquinia, the positions of buried tombs show up. The diagram on the right explains the photograph.

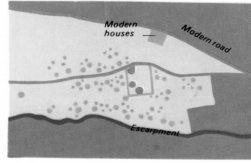

▨ Visible burial mounds
⋯ Tombs invisible from ground
▨ Cemetery area
▨ Plain

▲ Lerici makes a resistivity survey of an Etruscan graveyard. Once a tomb is located the mining drill behind will be used to bore a hole in the roof.

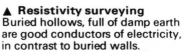

▲ **Resistivity surveying**
Buried hollows, full of damp earth are good conductors of electricity, in contrast to buried walls.

A resistivity meter, using needle-shaped electrodes, passes an electric current through the earth and then measures changes in the resistance of the soil caused by buried structures.

The Etruscan tombs

The Etruscans were artistic, fun-loving people who ruled Italy before the Romans. They buried their dead in painted underground tombs full of personal treasures.

Most of these tombs, like those of ancient Egypt, have been plundered by tomb robbers. The remainder are being rescued by archaeologists using air photography and other scientific methods that allow them to "see" underground.

The work was started by the Englishman John Bradford, who was able to study reconaissance photographs of Etruria taken by the R.A.F. during World War Two. Scores of new tombs, invisible on the ground, showed up as crop marks from the air.

The research was continued by the Italian industrial geologist, C. M. Lerici, who originally took up archaeology as a hobby. He found that he could adapt the methods geologists use when looking for minerals.

Tombs were discovered on the ground by instruments which detected underlying irregularities in the soil. Lerici then "looked" inside a tomb by boring a hole through the roof with a mining drill and then inserting a miniature camera and flash light on the end of a periscope.

▲ These three athletes are painted on the side of an Etruscan tomb at Caere. The painting dates from the end of the sixth century BC.

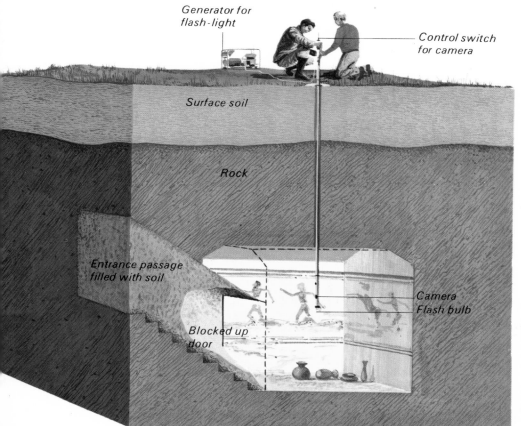

Generator for flash-light

Control switch for camera

Surface soil

Rock

Entrance passage filled with soil

Blocked up door

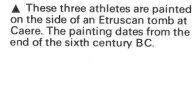

Camera
Flash bulb

◀ A tomb has been discovered and a hole drilled through the roof. Now Lerici inserts a metal tube containing a miniature camera and a flash light, both of which can be worked from ground level.

The camera is turned round to take different views of the inside of the tomb. These photographs will show Lerici if the tomb is worth excavating.

Tombs of the tyrants Chinese finds

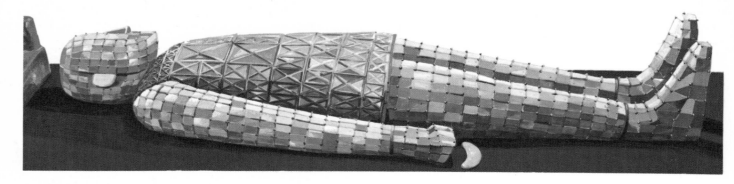

▲ Tou-Wan was dressed in a suit made of 2,156 tiny rectangular pieces of jade sewn together with gold thread. Such suits took years to make and only very rich nobles could afford them.

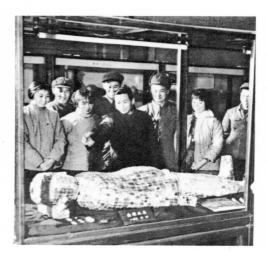

▲ Chinese people are looking at Liu Sheng's suit when it was on show shortly after being discovered.

▶ Real houses of the Han period have not survived but this model came from a tomb. Houses at this time were several storeys high with elaborate entrances, bright painted walls and tiled roofs.

Chinese archaeology

Unlike people in the West, who only became interested in archaeology recently, the Chinese have been enthusiastic archaeologists ever since the days of the Han emperors (206 BC onwards). Chinese scholars collected old manuscripts, drew and catalogued pottery and bronzes and left long descriptions of ancient cities.

In fact they did everything a modern archaeologist does except dig. It was not done for a scholar to get his hands dirty! The peasants were too poor, of course, to care about the past.

Since the communist revolution all this has changed. The state encourages excavations and tries to get everyone to take part: workers, farmers and soldiers. They have used their discoveries to show Chinese men and women how much better off they are today than when all China's wealth was owned by a very few people.

Rock-cut tombs

In 1968 Chinese soldiers discovered two rock-cut tombs carved out of the side of Mount Lingshan, and they called in the archaeologists. The tombs belonged to the Han prince Liu Sheng and his wife Tou-Wan. They were both wearing suits of jade and lay in huge underground halls surrounded by treasures, stores of food, chariots and horses.

After the funeral the priest had sealed the entrance passages with molten iron. The workmen may have been sacrificed to prevent the position of the tombs from becoming known.

A bronze lamp in Tou-Wan's tomb was made in the shape of a maid.

Pictures of the chariots from Liu Sheng's tomb have not been published. But they were probably similar to other chariot discoveries.
◀ These buried chariots had rotted away but their outlines were preserved in the sand.
▼ The horses were yoked to the chariot poles and must have half-strangled themselves when they pulled.

Archaeology in danger

Excavating cities

Many of the older cities in Europe are like Middle Eastern mounds. They are built on top of the ruins of much earlier towns dating back to medieval or Roman times or even earlier. Before the invention of bulldozers it was too difficult to root out these earlier foundations. It was simpler to level them and build on top.

It is difficult for the archaeologists to get at these earlier levels because of the modern buildings standing above them. Opportunities have to be seized as they arise. For instance, during World War Two, many European towns were flattened by bombing.

In London, archaeologists took advantage of the gaps left in the houses to recover the plans of the old Roman city and its more important buildings. Similar work took place on the continent at places like Trier and Cologne.

Now or never

More recently the older parts of many cities have been knocked down to make room for newer buildings. However, land in cities is very expensive and the construction companies cannot afford to hold up work for a long time while the archaeologists investigate.

Therefore many digs in cities, like that of Baynard's Castle in London, are "rescue excavations", carried out very rapidly in advance of the bulldozers.

Outside our present cities, too, historical sites are in danger of being lost. Constructions such as motorways and airports can destroy the sites of ancient country houses or villages.

Modern buildings are much higher and heavier than older ones and so they have to have much deeper foundations, going right down to bed-rock. If we do not excavate our ruins now, they will be bulldozed away for ever.

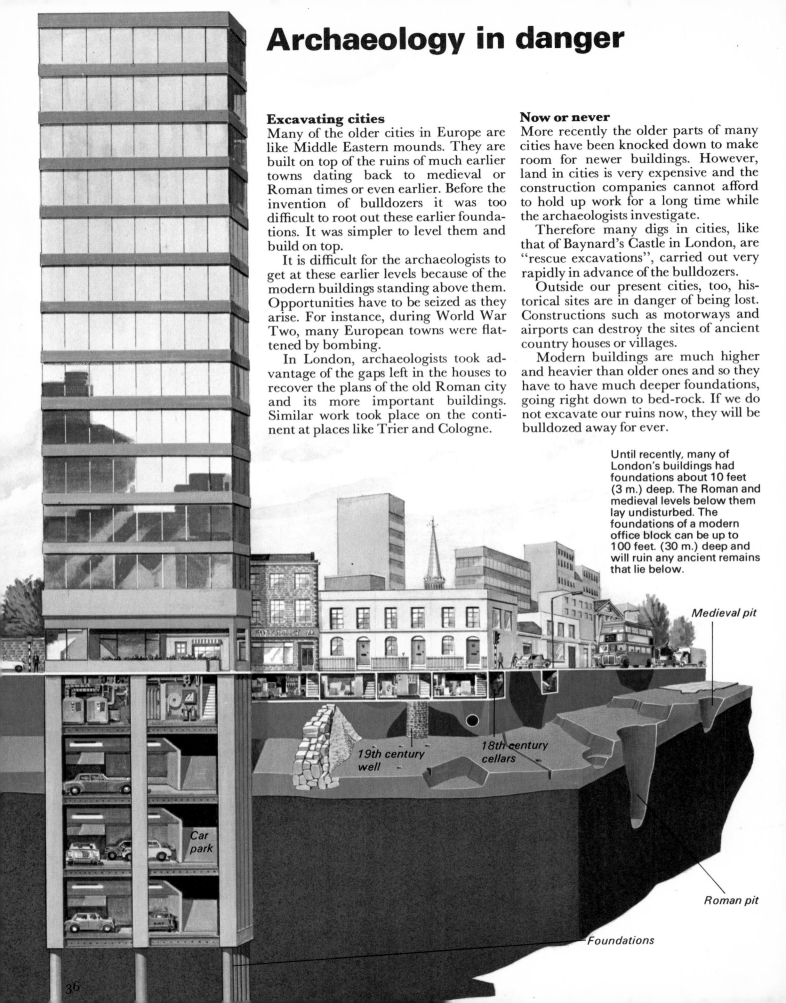

Until recently, many of London's buildings had foundations about 10 feet (3 m.) deep. The Roman and medieval levels below them lay undisturbed. The foundations of a modern office block can be up to 100 feet. (30 m.) deep and will ruin any ancient remains that lie below.

Medieval pit

19th century well

18th century cellars

Roman pit

Car park

Foundations

▼ Baynard's Castle was first built by Ralph Baynard, a friend of William the Conqueror. It was rebuilt in 1428 by the Duke of Gloucester, but was seized by the king when the duke was condemned for treason. It probably looked like this picture.

Old St Paul's Cathedral

▲ Henry VIII often held court at Baynard's Castle after it had been converted into a royal palace by his father Henry VII.

◄ Baynard's Castle was burnt down in 1666 when most of the City of London was destroyed in the Great Fire. Warehouses were built in its place.

► Now the warehouses, too, have been pulled down. New houses are going to be built and the huge bastion in the foreground will soon be covered by a road filled with heavy traffic. Before the building takes place, however, the archaeologists move in and excavate the old castle.

The vanishing present industrial archaeology

The pot shop
Clay pots called crucibles were made here. A mould was filled with clay and a plug hammered down into the centre, hollowing it out. The pot was then fired.

Archaeology in a changing world
Archaeology is not always about civilizations of the long distant past. Industrial archaeologists have realized that within the last two centuries our own civilization has been rapidly changing.

Man has completely altered his way of working and travelling since the Industrial Revolution. Buildings like windmills that were previously used for work have been replaced by factories, and horse-drawn vehicles are now seldom seen. The machines within the industries themselves are also constantly changing and falling into disuse.

It is the job of an industrial archaeologist to preserve and record examples of old machinery, factories and methods of transport before they are lost.

Industrial museums are often related to a local industry. In England, Sheffield has long been the centre for making steel for tools and cutlery.

At Abbeydale Industrial Hamlet, Sheffield, you can see how men made steel scythe blades 200 years ago. Today the work is very different. Without industrial archaeologists our recent past would become as remote as the civilizations of Troy or Peru.

The fitting shop
The blades and handles were finally assembled, ready for sale. Later the shop was converted to make a new type of scythe.

The charge room
Here the crude steel or iron used for crucible steel making was broken up, weighed into portions and mixed with the right amounts of charcoal to form "charges."

The water wheels
Water from the River Shear was used to turn the huge wooden wheels which worked the tilt-hammer and grindstones.

The crucible steel furnace
The "charges" were put into crucibles which were then placed in the "melting holes" of the crucible steel furnace and melted for four hours at about 1,550° C.

Teeming
At the end of the "melt", the pots were removed from the furnace and workmen called "teemers" poured the molten steel into moulds.

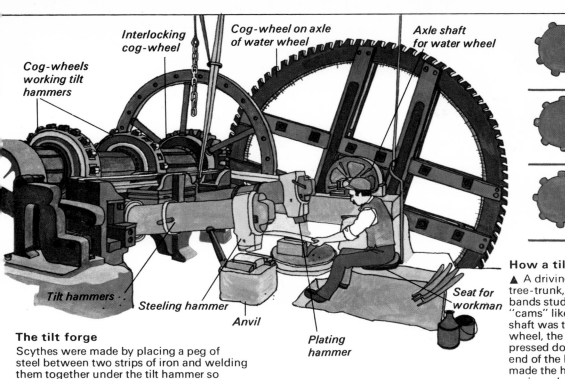

Cog-wheels working tilt hammers

Interlocking cog-wheel

Cog-wheel on axle of water wheel

Axle shaft for water wheel

Tilt hammers

Steeling hammer

Anvil

Plating hammer

Seat for workman

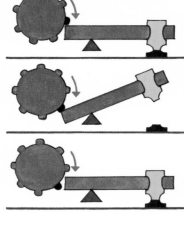

How a tilt-hammer works

▲ A driving shaft, made from a tree-trunk, was fitted with iron bands studded with small lumps or "cams" like a dog collar. As the shaft was turned by the water-wheel, the "cams" alternately pressed down and released the end of the hammer-shaft. This made the hammer-head fall back again and again on to the anvil.

The tilt forge
Scythes were made by placing a peg of steel between two strips of iron and welding them together under the tilt hammer so that the steel formed the cutting edge.

The boring shop
Here the scythe-blades were prepared to receive their handles, which were turned on a lathe in the work-shop next door.

The grinding shop
Grinding was well-paid but unpleasant. As the grind-stones turned round they threw grit and sparks into the grinders' eyes, and sometimes the wheels exploded, killing the workmen.

◀ At the Henry Ford Museum in Michigan, U.S. you can study anything from miners' lamps to jet engines. Here, a 1905 Ford Model "F", a 1903 Ford model "A" and a 1901 Ford prototype stand at the first factory of the Ford Motor Company.

▼ Henry Ford built his first automobile, the "quadricycle", in his back yard in 1896 when he was 33.

Archaeological sites

Mexico City:
Aztec site
(p. 28–29)

Indian pueblos
(p. 20–21)

Tollund
(p. 15)

Machu Picchu
(p. 30–31)

Mochica area
(p. 30–31)

Paracas area
(p. 30–31)

Sheffield: Abbeyvale
Industrial Hamlet
(p. 38—39)

London: Baynard's Castle
(p. 36–37)

The map shows the position of
some of the archaeological sites
mentioned in this book. Of course
there are thousands of others all
over the world but there has not
been room to describe them all.

Tarquinia: Etruscan tombs
(p. 32–33)

Pompeii
(p. 4–5)

King Zoser's
Step Pyramid
(p. 8–9)

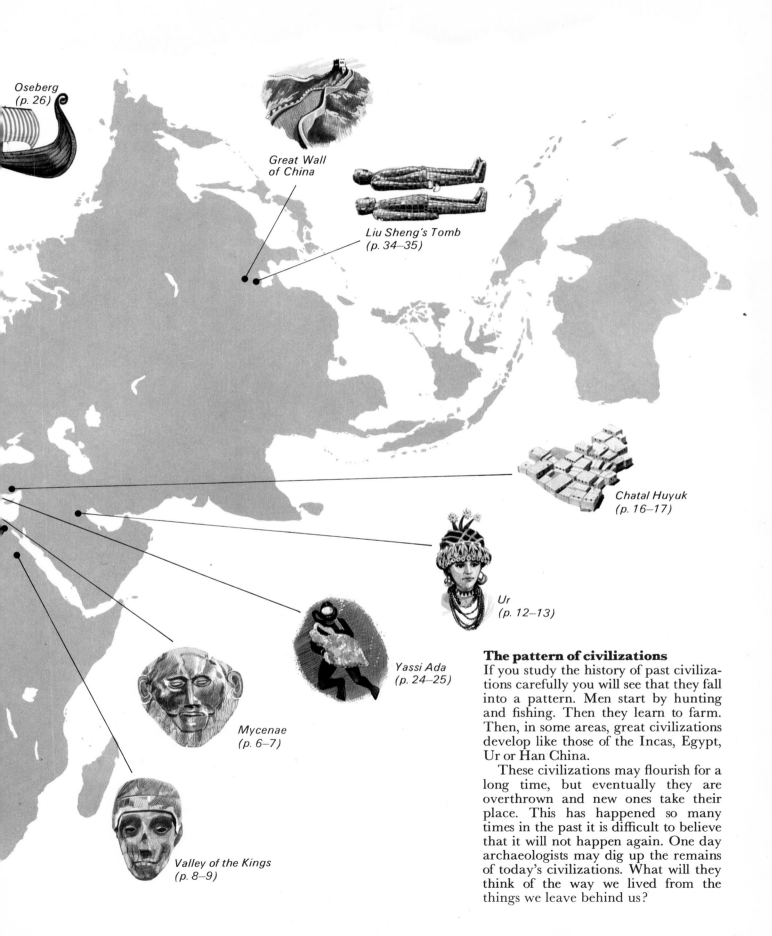

Oseberg
(p. 26)

Great Wall
of China

Liu Sheng's Tomb
(p. 34–35)

Chatal Huyuk
(p. 16–17)

Ur
(p. 12–13)

Yassi Ada
(p. 24–25)

Mycenae
(p. 6–7)

Valley of the Kings
(p. 8–9)

The pattern of civilizations

If you study the history of past civilizations carefully you will see that they fall into a pattern. Men start by hunting and fishing. Then they learn to farm. Then, in some areas, great civilizations develop like those of the Incas, Egypt, Ur or Han China.

These civilizations may flourish for a long time, but eventually they are overthrown and new ones take their place. This has happened so many times in the past it is difficult to believe that it will not happen again. One day archaeologists may dig up the remains of today's civilizations. What will they think of the way we lived from the things we leave behind us?

Projects models and rubbings

Collecting brass rubbings

In parts of Europe, but particularly in Germany, Belgium and England, you will see rectangular brass plaques in the floor of churches. They are carved with portraits of bishops, knights and ladies, and are memorials to people of the Middle Ages.

You can copy these brasses by making rubbings of them.

The best materials to use are black heel-ball and architect's detail paper, which you can buy at an art shop. But it also works using coloured wax crayons and lining papers for walls.

You will need a soft decorators' paint brush, some clean bits of rag for dusters, sticky tape (the sort called "masking tape" that does not leave dirty marks behind it), scissors, a note book and a pencil.

If you want to rub a brass on the floor of a church, you must first get permission from the vicar or church warden. Kneel down beside the brass; never stand or kneel on it.

Clean up the surface with your paint brush and rags. Use the toothbrush to remove any grits from the engraved outlines. Be careful not to scratch the brass.

Smooth the paper over the brass and stick down the corners. Then start to rub, working from one end of the plaque to the other and using a firm even pressure. Always use the side of the heel-ball or crayon.

▲ This picture shows the tools and method used for brass rubbing.

▶ This rubbing shows Sir Thomas Bullen, the father of Henry VIII's second wife, Ann Boleyn.

Rubbings in general

There are plenty of things to rub besides church brasses. In central America archaeologists use rubbings to record Maya stone reliefs. In China they rub tomb-carvings. But if you live in a big city anywhere, you can copy man-hole covers and gravestones.

Rubbings can be stored as they are or the figure can be cut out and mounted on thicker paper. If you fix the top of the paper to a wooden rod and tie a picture cord to the ends, it makes a good wall hanging.

Making a cylinder seal

In the ancient Middle East, where people wrote on clay tablets, they signed their letters with a personal seal. This was a small cylinder of stone or clay carved with pictures of men, gods or animals. When the cylinder was rolled across the clay it left a raised picture behind. To make a cylinder seal you need:

A candle;
A sharp pointed knife;
A rolling pin or milk bottle;
Plasticine.

Mark off a piece of candle about $1\frac{1}{2}$ ins (40 mm.) long and carve a design on it running round the side. Start with a simple pattern, and then try more complicated designs. Slice off the candle end.

Roll out a piece of plasticine to make a flat block about 2 by 6 ins (50 by 150 mm.). Starting at one end roll your seal carefully across it, taking care to press evenly the whole time. If it tends to stick to the plasticine, dust the seal with a little talcum powder.

Making a stamp seal

A simpler type of seal was the "stamp seal" often attached to a signet ring. There are some beautiful examples from Crete showing animals, and warriors fighting.

To make a stamp seal, carve a design on the *end* of a candle and press it on to your plasticine block. If you use a thick candle you will have room for quite an elaborate design.

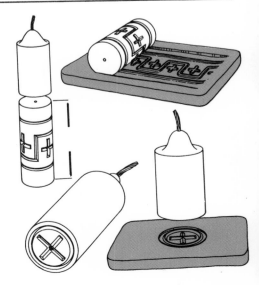

Making a model village

This is how to make a model of a camp of European hunters in about 8000 BC (as described on page 14).

Make the back and base of your model from two pieces of hardboard, or use the lid and base of a cardboard box (Fig. A).

Paint a picture of a wintry landscape with a marshy area in front dotted with clumps of birch trees. Stick it to your back-drop (Fig. B).

Fasten a piece of mirror or ripple glass to the front of the base to represent a lake, and cover the rest of the base with earth or plasticine covered with moss. Stick birch twigs into the ground for trees, and spread small twigs around to look like a brushwood platform (Fig. C).

The people who lived on the edge of the lake would have had long hair and beards and worn skins. They lived by hunting red deer, elk and small game. You may be able to find small plastic models of men and animals you can adapt, or you can use plasticine or make cardboard cut-outs. You can also make figures out of pipe-cleaners, flesh-coloured bias-binding and wool (Fig. D).

Arm the men with match-stick harpoons (Fig. E). Place one fishing on the lake from a dug-out canoe made from balsa-wood. Two others can be chopping down a tree with axes made from match sticks and plasticine. Make a lean-to shelter of twigs against a tree and put a woman outside it near a "fire" of red paper.

Now you can make other similar settlements. Try to copy pictures or descriptions from archaeology books.

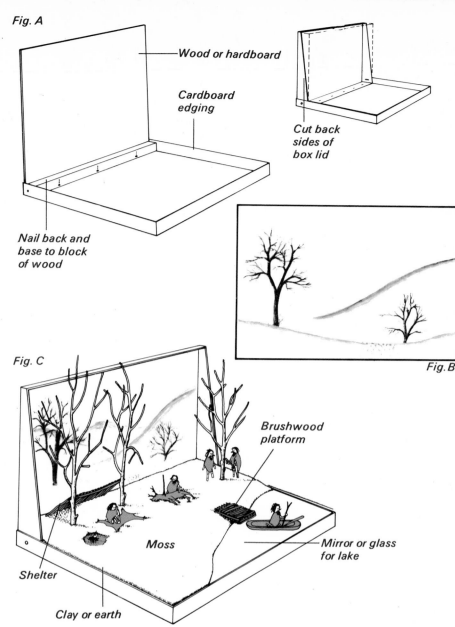

Fig. A

Wood or hardboard

Cardboard edging

Cut back sides of box lid

Nail back and base to block of wood

Fig. B

Fig. C

Brushwood platform

Moss

Mirror or glass for lake

Shelter

Clay or earth

Making figures

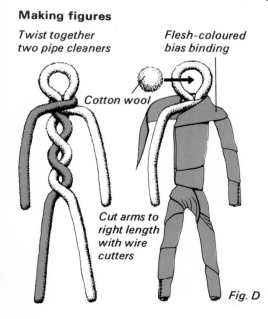

Twist together two pipe cleaners

Flesh-coloured bias binding

Cotton wool

Cut arms to right length with wire cutters

Fig. D

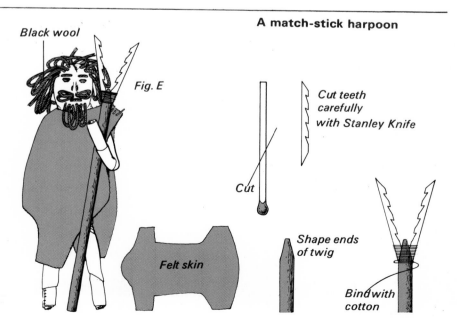

Black wool

Fig. E

Felt skin

A match-stick harpoon

Cut teeth carefully with Stanley Knife

Cut

Shape ends of twig

Bind with cotton

Project surveying your site

Making a plane table

One of the most important parts of archaeology is surveying and planning a site. For this, the archaeologist needs a plane table and an alidade. These are quite easy to make.

The table is a 15 in. (400 mm.) square cut from veneered chipboard. For the leg, you want a 48 in. (1200 mm.) length of straight, hard-grained wood about ½ in. (12 mm.) square. Taper one end of the leg to a point. (Fig. A).

Fasten the table to the top of the leg using two small metal angle brackets and screws. Make sure that the leg comes in the centre of the table bottom and that the table is square with the leg. Cut two triangular braces about 4 in. (100 mm.) on each side and glue these to the leg and table bottom, on opposite sides to give a really firm mounting.

Two large metal angle brackets are then screwed on opposite sides of the leg 12 in. (300 mm.) from the bottom, as shown. These will steady the table and keep the leg vertical when the end is pushed into the ground.

Alternatively, a camera tripod could be adapted to make the leg. Cut a square of fairly thick plywood and drill a hole through the centre to make a tight fit on the tripod screw (Fig. B). Then screw the ply onto the tripod and screw and glue the table to this firm base.

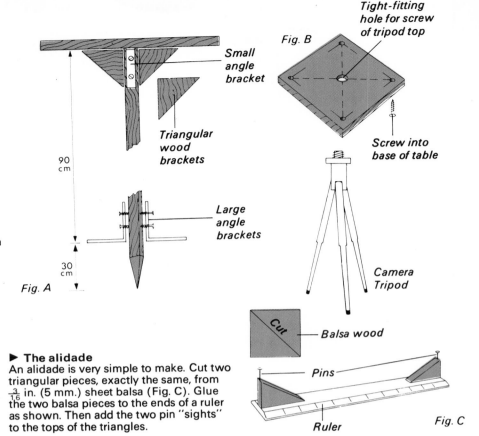

Fig. B

Tight-fitting hole for screw of tripod top

Small angle bracket

Triangular wood brackets

Large angle brackets

90 cm

30 cm

Fig. A

Screw into base of table

Camera Tripod

Cut — Balsa wood

Pins

Ruler

Fig. C

▶ The alidade

An alidade is very simple to make. Cut two triangular pieces, exactly the same, from $\frac{3}{16}$ in. (5 mm.) sheet balsa (Fig. C). Glue the two balsa pieces to the ends of a ruler as shown. Then add the two pin "sights" to the tops of the triangles.

Working out heights

Here is a rough and ready way of working out the height of an earth-work, like a burial mound or castle motte. You need a piece of hardboard or ply about 2ft. (0.5 m.) square.

First find out your eye level by sticking a tape-measure to the edge of a door and standing in front of it. It is helpful if you can make it a round number, like 5 ft. or 1.50 m. Then go to the bottom of your earth-work.

Place the board to your eye and site along it horizontally. This gives you the position of your eye level on the earth-work (Point A). Note its position in relation to a flower or tuft of grass or get a friend to stand there.

Then climb till you are standing on Point A and take a new siting to find your new eye level. The height of the earth-work is the sum of the number of eye levels plus the measurement left over at the top.

Making a tape-measure

The best sort of tape-measure to use is the type about 25 yards or 20 or 25 metres long which rolls up into a leather case. You can, however, make a substitute from a ball of tough white string.

Tie a curtain ring firmly to one end of the string and hook it over something firm. Then stretch the string across the room and pull it taut.

Using an ordinary tape-measure, mark in your yards or metres with tags tied on very tightly. Draw in the sub-divisions with ink dots. You can judge the smaller measurements by eye when you are doing the actual planning, or use a ruler. Keep the curtain ring at the end of the string to hold on to.

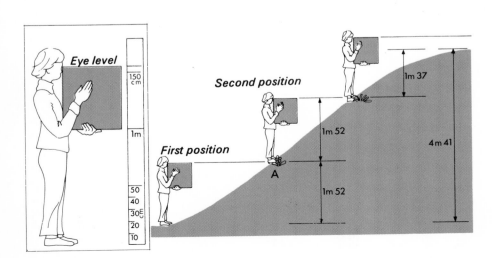

Eye level

150 cm

1m

50
40
30
20
10

First position

Second position

A

1m 37

1m 52

1m 52

4m 41

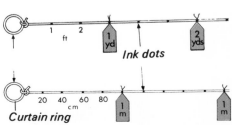

Ink dots

ft 1 2

1 yd

2 yds

Curtain ring

20 40 60 80 cm

1 m

1 m

Using the plane table

Start by planning your garden. You need a friend as a helper, a long pole, a tape-measure at least 20 yards (20 metres) long, an accurate ruler, a builders' level, a small compass and a pin.

Cover the top of the plane table with paper and set it up in the middle of the garden. Level the top. Then decide on the scale you want to use. Convenient ones are $\frac{1}{4}$ or $\frac{1}{2}$ in. to 1 ft., or 20 or 50 mm. to 1 metre. Stick the pin into the centre of the board. This is the position of the table on your plan.

Plan your garden

Give your friend one end of the tape and send him to stand with the pole on the first point to be plotted, in, for example, the far right hand corner of the garden. Pivot your alidade against the pin and squint down it until the two pins each end of the alidade line up with the pole.

Draw a line in the direction of the pole along the side of the alidade. Then measure the distance between the centre pin and the pole and mark this off on your plan to the correct scale, e.g. at 20 mm. to 1 metre, 10.3 metres would be 206 mm.

Then send your friend to the next point, another corner of the garden, and do the same thing again. Now join the points of the two corners up and you have the line of your hedge. Continue round the garden plotting all the main features, such as the position of trees and flower beds.

You can sketch in the smaller details by eye or with the aid of a ruler when the main outline is finished. If, by mistake, you jog your board, line it up with the alidade on one of the points you have alrea drawn in. Finally put in the position of north with your compass.

Large areas

If you want to plan an area larger than about 30–40 yards (27–36 metres) across, you will have to plan the two halves separately. But make sure that several features in the middle overlap so that you can join the plans up afterwards.

Finally, back at home, put a clean piece of tracing paper over your plan and make a fair copy in ink, without all the guide lines. Add the scale, the north point, the name of the area planned and the date you did it.

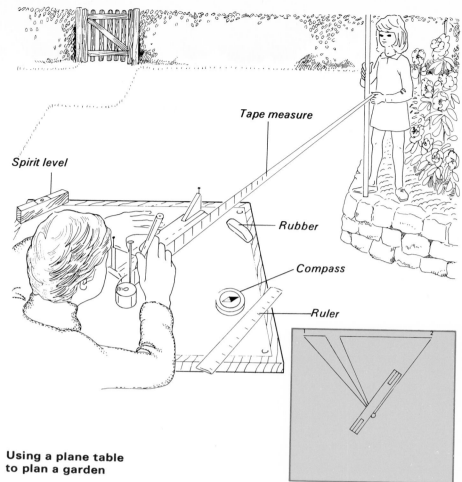

Spirit level

Tape measure

Rubber

Compass

Ruler

Using a plane table to plan a garden

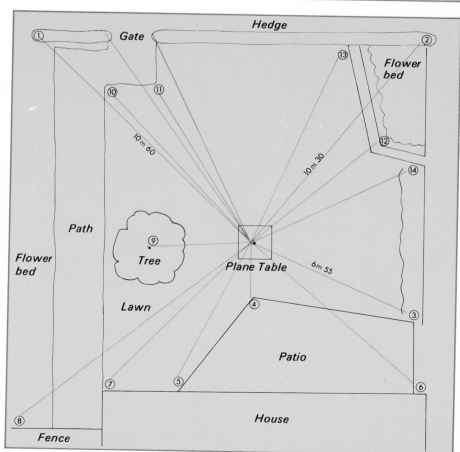

Reference

What to do next

Get to know your own area

Most of you will probably not live near a site like Pompeii. On the other hand very few areas of the Old World and America do not have some form of ancient remains.

Old Stone Age: Caves.

New Stone Age: Long barrows, chambered cairns, causewayed camps.

Bronze Age: Round barrows, stone circles and "Henge monuments" like Stonehenge, hut circles.

Iron Age: Hill forts, Celtic fields, ancient track ways.

Roman: Roman cities and roads.

Medieval: Castles and castle mounds, deserted villages and old field systems, wayside crosses.

If you visit an ancient site and walk carefully over the ground looking in rabbit scrapes or areas that have been newly ploughed, you may be lucky enough to find a flint arrowhead or piece of pottery.

Try to find out if there are any old factories operating in your area, or if anything interesting is turning up on a local building site.

Visit a local museum

Many museums now have someone specially appointed to deal with queries from young people. Your museum should be able to tell you what to look for in your area, what has already been found there, and whether there is any field work going on that you can take part in.

Help on an excavation

Local museums and universities also run excavations and need volunteers to do the digging. At first you will not be given very much responsibility but will work under the direction of a more experienced "site supervisor". It is worth learning to do one of the specialized excavation tasks such as photography, planning or drawing small finds and pots.

If your local museum is not running anything write to:

The Council for British Archaeology, 8 St. Andrew's Place, London NW1 4LB.

The Council publishes a Calendar of Excavations which is sent to members for an annual subscription of 80p. Always join a professionally run dig. Never dig on your own.

For 50p you can join an organization called Young Rescue which is run by Kate Pretty, New Hall, Cambridge.

Members receive a badge and a membership card which allows them to visit archaeological sites not normally open to the public.

Books

The books which appear at the top of this list are easier.

Introducing Archaeology, *by Magnus Magnusson, (Bodley Head)*

The Archaeology of Ancient Egypt, *by T. G. H. James, (Bodley Head)*

Archaeology; an illustrated introduction, *by Liam de Paor, (Pelican)*

The Testimony of the Spade, *by G. Bibby, (Fontana)*

The Young Field Archaeologist's Guide, *by J. X. W. P. Corcoran, (G. Bell & Sons)*

Prehistoric Britain, *by Barbara Green & Alan Sorrell, (Lutterworth Press)*

Roman Britain, *by Aileen Fox & Alan Sorrell, (Lutterworth Press)*

Regional Archaeologies, Yorkshire, The Severn Basin, North Wales, South Wales, South West Scotland, The Roman Frontiers of Britain & Wessex, *series edited by D. M. Wilson, (Heinemann Educational Books)*

Everyday Life in the Viking Age, *by Jacqueline Simpson, (Transworld)*

Larousse Encyclopaedia of Archaeology, *(Hamlyn)*

Earliest Civilizations of the Near East, *by James Mellaart, (Thames & Hudson)*

Early Civilization in China, *by William Watson, (Thames & Hudson)*

The First Americans, *by G. S. Bushnell, (Thames & Hudson)*

The Royal Hordes, *by E. D. Phillips, (Thames & Hudson)*

Archaeology Under Water, *by G. S. Bass, (Thames & Hudson)*

Gods, Graves & Scholars, *by C. W. Ceram, (Gollancz)*

Field Archaeology, *by R. J. C. Atkinson, (Methuen & Co Ltd.)*

Archaeology, Dictionary of, *David Trump & Warwick Bray, (Penguin)*

Glossary

amulet a charm worn against evil.

bronze a metal made by alloying copper with a small proportion of tin. Before men discovered how to work iron it was used for most tools.

carnelian a dull red stone.

citadel a high fortress overlooking a city.

civilization means literally "living in cities". In history, people are said to be civilized when they stop living in small farming communities and start organizing themselves into large groups under a proper government.

corrode to decay, wear away (usually of metal).

corrosion the decay on the surface of a piece of metal.

embalm, mummify to preserve a dead body from decay either by treating it with herbs or by drying it.

engrave to carve or scratch lines in a hard surface.

excavate to dig out.

excavation (also known as a "dig") the work of uncovering archaeological sites.

find the name used for any object found during a dig.

fresco a wall painting done while the plaster background is still damp.

gunwale the upper edge of the side of a boat.

inlay, inlaid precious stones or pieces of metal set in a background.

inscription any piece of writing but usually one carved on stone.

jade a very hard blue or green stone.

lapis lazuli a dark blue stone.

level an instrument that looks like a small telescope revolving on top of a tripod. It is used with a long folding staff marked off in fractions of a metre or yard to **take levels** i.e. find out the heights of structures discovered on a dig.

manuscript a hand-written book or letter.

Mesopotamia modern Iraq.

Metric staff a rod, 2 metres long, painted alternately in red and white bands, used in archaeological planning and photography.

reconstruct an object to try to restore it to the way it looked in the past.

reconstruct events to work out what might have happened in the past.

site place where ancient remains are found.

shrine a chapel or holy place.

Index

Illustration Credits